Espresso Cappuccino & Co

Espressum

Author: Markus J.M. Bihler
Project Management: Barbara Ehniß
Photography: Otto Kasper Studios
Graphic Design: Horst Schroff
Graphics p. 20–23: Atelier Urban
Prepress: CIRCUS imaging ARTists
Print: Karl Wolf Offsetdruck
Published by: CIRCUS imaging ARTists

English Translation: Alf W. Mildenberger
English Editors: Tony N. Bernstein, Linda Boro

Espresso - Italians use this word to describe the art of coffee preparation and drinking. It actually means "fast", "quick", "rush" and "dynamic", referring to the brewing of the coffee itself, and not the hectic and stressful life of today. On the contrary, the refined art of enjoying an espresso is reason for a break to think and reflect, relax, lay back and enjoy!

Many wonderful books have been written about nostalgic Italian Coffee Bars, Viennese Coffeehouses as well as the history, development and evolution of espresso machines. For the true coffee aficionado, these books provide all of the interesting information, however, they are usually too detailed and therefore not likely to be read. This book has an entirely different purpose. It is informative and offers comprehensive information about the art of espresso preparation, written in a format that is reflective of the act of relaxing and enjoying life. It also deals with certain myths and misinformation that have been in circulation as long as the artform of espresso.

Not every espresso deserves to be called an espresso. Too many do not live up to its well deserved reputation. Who better to establish the standards for espresso than the Italian baristi, the coffee roasters and machine manufacturers? They are the true experts in the field, and this book relies heavily on their collective expertise, gathered over many years of tradition and genuine passion.

Many questions have been posed to me over the numerous years that I have personally been in the coffee industry. Let me try and give you the answers to those questions, as we together explore the true pleasures and passion associated with espresso.

Markus J.M. Bihler

Origin and geography.

The world of coffee.

Most topics have their myths and legends, and coffee is filled with these also. Earliest references to coffee that we have relate back in time to the land of Yemen in North Africa. The first time that coffee was produced on a larger scale was in today's Ethiopia, and one of the coffee producing provinces in Ethiopia is still called Mocha.

Neighboring Arab countries soon discovered the stimulating and seductive powers of coffee and started roasting coffee beans on stone plates. The name "coffee" has its origin in the Arab word "Kahwe", which means strength and power.

Coffee, well liked for its wonderful flavor, aroma and stimulating power comes from 80 known botanical varieties, of which only the "coffea arabica" known as Arabica, and the "coffea canephora" known as Robusta are economically viable for coffee production.

The Arabica bean with an oval form and a slightly curved cut is very climate sensitive. It grows best in average temperatures ranging from 55 to 90 degrees F and altitudes between 2,400 and 3,600 feet. That's why Arabica is also often referred to as high-grown or highland coffee. The main producing areas are countries in Central and South America, East Africa, India and Indonesia. The caffeine content in Arabica is lower than in Robusta. The sophisticated flavors vary in parameters of fine and noble nuances of acidity with a full body and a slightly exotic taste that is reminiscent of a hint of chocolate. The crema of Arabica has a deep red-brown color.

The species of Robusta was only discovered about 100 years ago. It differentiates from Arabica by its more round shape and a straight cut. Robusta beans with their heartier trees are not as climate sensitive and are usually grown in lower altitudes in West Africa and the Far East. These conditions lend to more economical cultivation, resulting in lower market prices. They are stronger and more full bodied in flavor than the Arabica beans, exhibiting a warm grey-brown crema.

That´s what good Espre

The simple secrets of its preparation.

Small, strong, hot, with a heavenly taste and its crema initially supporting the sugar, that then slowly sinks to the bottom of the cup. This represents a mirror image of Italian lifestyle, full of vitality, temperament and sophistication. It punctuates our everyday life with moments of sweetness and stimulates our mind. Take a break from your daily hectic activities and discover the true pleasures of espresso, savoring that rich aroma, sweet taste and creative mind journey... Often people think that making a good espresso seems to be a science of its own. In reality, it is a lot less complicated than one would think at first glance. Some basic knowledge and a few prerequisites are all that you need to experience the joy of espresso in your home.

Of course, pleasure as a concept is very subjective. But – there are some fundamental basic requirements, which are the quality of water, the choice of coffee beans, the corresponding machine and the preparation thereof. These ingredients form the basis of quality espresso.

The full bodied blend, rich and seductive aroma with slightly oily consistency provide the pleasure to the coffee lover. A good espresso is always recognized by its rich crema covering the coffee. This perfect crema will protect the ethereal aromas from evaporating. As espresso is considered the heart of coffee, the crema is its soul!

It is this rich, dense foam of golden brown and slightly marbleized appearance that denotes quality. Crema too light in color that dissipates rapidly is an indication that various components have not been sufficiently released. Crema too dark in color with a white spot or a hole in the middle is indicative of coffee that is burned or brewed too hot.

SO looks like!

Since life is too short to drink bad coffee, the
guidelines of this book are meant to lead the way
to true coffee quality...

Cappuccino:

The art of making good milk froth.

Cappuccino, although one of America's most popular drinks, is mainly served in restaurants and coffee bars, but less so in homes, because it is often perceived to be too difficult and complicated. The preparation of steamed milk seems as much a secret to cappuccino as is a good crema to espresso. The taste of the cappuccino is also influenced by the correct ratio of milk to espresso. All of this sounds very confusing, doesn't it? It need not be, and in reality it is quite simple, provided you have the correct ingredients and proper equipment.

The classic cappuccino recipe calls for three equal parts of espresso, milk and froth, but never cream. It is the milk froth that crowns the espresso like a cap. Hence the name, which derives from the Italian word for the hood on the Capuchin monk's dress, called "cappuccio".

The monk´s espresso.

The froth needs to be firm enough to support the sugar momentarily before it descends into the cup, much in the same way as good crema functions in an espresso.

The art of effective milk steaming is the subject of many "heated" debates, but once again, the correct ingredients, equipment and some basic skills are all that is needed for you to enjoy cappuccino in your own home.

Of utmost importance is a quality espresso machine that is capable of generating sufficient steam. Skim milk or low fat content milk are needed, as is a sizeable stainless steel milk pitcher. Be aware that the volume of the milk will increase when steamed! The steam outlet of the machine needs to be submerged just below the surface of the milk, and the pitcher must be moved slightly up and down, capturing the air and creating the foam. The milk should never boil and the temperature of the pitcher must be such that it can still be touched by a naked hand. The steamed milk should rest for a while, so that the foam can firm up and remain on the espresso for a longer period of time.

The Blender´s Secrets.

Masterpieces of composition for refined taste.

Coffee is shipped from the producing countries in sisal or burlap bags, and at that stage is called green coffee. Only in the land of destination does it go through the processes of blending and roasting, which are possible to be done in either sequence, depending on the roast and blend master's own recipe. The aim is to achieve a result of harmonically balanced taste and continuous, uniform quality over time.

Coffee roasters buy green coffee from various countries and regions in order to create their own blend. There are more than seventy producing countries in the world and each country has different qualities from different regions that offer a vast variety of taste characteristics. One can imagine that it takes enormous understanding and experience by the blend masters, to purchase the right green beans with the matching characteristics to create a blend of coffee that meets the exacting standards of coffee lovers in a specific market. Only years of learning and trying will lead to blends that stay constantly satisfying and unique, much as this is true for creating good wines and excellent champagnes. The exact recipes are the strictly guarded secrets of the roasters and their blend masters.

In Italy, the home of espresso, traditional blends were made of approximately 60 % Arabica and 40 % Robusta beans. The trend of late has become to use up to 100 % Arabica beans, as the preferences seem to have moved to more complex acidity with rich aroma, while some roasters decided to stick with their more traditional blends.

Eventually, it is up to the individual coffee lover to decide which coffee to enjoy and appreciate.

Hot Beans
Great Flavor.

Roasting -
The ultimate processing of coffee.

Coffee contains close to 800 flavor components. It is only the roasting process that releases these components and so creates an incredible complexity of aromatic taste.

The exact process is determined by each coffee roaster, but generally the green coffee is placed into a roasting machine that runs at high temperatures of 450 – 500 degrees F for between 2 – 10 minutes, depending on the roasting system used to transform the green coffee bean into the roasted bean. Traditional roasting machines work with a rotating hot bin, while modern equipment often uses a hot air stream for the same process. It is during this roasting process that the green bean looses much of its water and so experiences a considerable weight loss, while at the same time expanding to almost double the original size. This occurs because of the evaporation of water and subsequent gases that develop within the bean itself.

The length of the roasting process is critical to the final flavor of the coffee. The longer the roasting time, the darker the bean becomes and correspondingly, the stronger the flavor. Espresso beans are roasted longer than "regular" coffee, which among other things lets them loose some of the acids that tend to be aggressive to the stomach.

Dark roasts exhibit an oily film on their outside, called ethereal oils. It is these ethereal oils that carry the flavor and help build and maintain the desired crema - the espresso's true soul.

Coffee Freshly Ground.

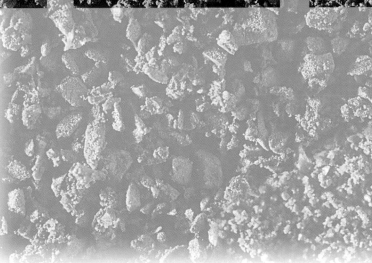

Grinding – The key to aroma.

One important step in achieving a good cup of coffee is the grinding of the beans. It is only ground coffee that finally releases its full and true flavor, and once in contact with the hot water, develops its ultimate character. Therefore, coffee once ground, is subject to a loss of flavor and quality. This is why it is preferable to grind the beans freshly, just prior to brewing. One alternative, becoming increasingly popular, is the coffee pouch or pod and this method will be discussed in a later section.

Of course the actual method of grinding is of great importance, and the degree of grinding will ultimately influence the flavor and quality in the cup. The grind has to match the brewing system and only when both systems work in total harmony, will a full flavored cup be the end result.

Each method of coffee brewing requires a different degree of grinding. Turkish mocha requires the finest possible and powderlike grind. A fine grind is needed for espresso brewed with a pressure pump machine. For filter or drip coffee, medium grinding is advisable, and for French press a coarse grind. To select the correct adjustment on the scale of a grinder, one must know that usually the higher numbers indicate a coarser grind, and the lower numbers will give you the finer grind.

It´s just simple
Coffee Pods.

Single serving portions
– a clever alternative.

Traditionally, the preparation of espresso requires the coffee beans to be freshly ground prior to brewing. The coffee powder is then packed into the filter basket and lightly tamped. The handling of coffee powder, however, can be somewhat messy. In order to simplify espresso brewing the very convenient coffee pod has been developed. These pods offer a single serving of espresso, where the coffee is ground to perfection and hermetically packed, preserving the aroma and great taste. Immediately after grinding, oxygen is withdrawn from the coffee powder and nitrogen is infused, making the coffee free from oxidation and ensuring long shelf life. This assures the coffee is as good as the day it was ground.

These pods are predominantly made of filter paper, although some are made of aluminum or plastic. They are placed into the filter holder and disposed after every serving use.
The standards for this product have been set by an international coffee roasters association and are standardized through the Easy Serving Espresso guidelines (ESE).
This revolutionary discovery enables for simpler handling and great tasting espresso every time without any inconvenience!

The
Classic.

Original lovor maohinoo.

The true classic is a manual espresso machine. These piston lever machines reflect the early individualistic art of the basic espresso brewing technique, and form the basis of all modern equipment today.

Pressure is generated by manually pressing the lever in a downward motion, creating approximately 140 psi of pressure, which is adequate for the perfect espresso.

The famous La Pavoni espresso machine is considered the most outstanding example, both in design and function and is housed in the Museum of Modern Art in New York.

One should remember that these machines do require some expertise and practice in perfecting the technique, but they are decorative as well as functional, although missing some of the convenience of more modern equipment.

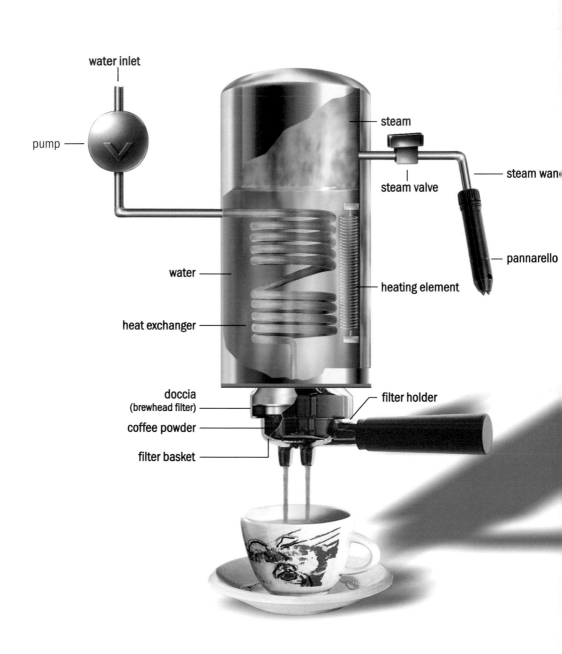

water inlet

pump

steam

steam valve

steam wand

pannarello

water

heating element

heat exchanger

doccia
(brewhead filter)

coffee powder

filter basket

filter holder

What it takes is pressure.

Traditional espresso technology.

As we already have stated, the making of good espresso is more than just a simple mechanical act – it is a ritual!

The quality and flavor, taste and aroma of this delightful little pleasure are dictated by the pressure generated by the internal pump in the machine, as well as the correct grind of coffee, and the method in which this coffee is packed into the filter basket. If the coffee is ground too coarse and not pressed down adequately, the water will pass by without building up enough pressure and the espresso will be weak, lacking flavor and aroma. If the grind is too fine or there is too much coffee in the filter basket, the flow of water is restricted and the coffee will only drip through. This leads to an unsatisfying taste and no crema building up. The classic method of espresso brewing requires pressure that is produced by a pump, but not by steam. Steam is only utilized to froth milk for cappuccino. In the procedure, fresh water is pumped into a boiler and heated up. The ground coffee in the filter basket is lightly tamped and the filter holder attached to the machine. Now the pump presses the hot water through the ground coffee and thereby extracts the "heart of coffee", a perfect cup of espresso.

It is dispensed in pre-heated cups and if grind and pressure are at their optimum, the espresso should take no more or less than 20 to 25 seconds to brew, hence the name association with "quick" and "fast".

Thermostats keep the boiler temperature of pump driven household espresso machines at a brewing temperature of 195 degrees F and at steam temperature of 260 degrees F. The flow temperature of the water, which is measured where the water meets the coffee, is to be about 175 to 180 degrees F. The ideal water pressure produced by the pump is between 140 psi. The power of the pump in the espresso machine itself is a critical component to the enjoyment of the drink.

The ground coffee is only in contact with the water for a very short period of time, and the result is a cup of coffee that exhibits far less caffeine, acids and bitter aroma than is found in traditional filter or drip coffee. It is this special brewing method that makes drinking espresso the delectable experience it is!

Modern times.

State of the art espresso machines.

Today's modern espresso machines are able to achieve the quality standards that are set by the Italian baristi. One of the basic requirement is, that these machines incorporate an electrical pump with a nominal pressure capacity of about 200 to 230 psi. A machine without this prerequisite does not qualify.

The actual pressure that is used to extract an espresso at its best is about 140 psi. It is determined by how fine the coffee is ground and pressed into the filter basket. A coarse and uncompressed grind will let the water run through without building up pressure. A too fine grind that is compressed too strongly will not let the water penetrate at all. Today's household espresso machines produce hot water and steam with boilers that are made of brass, stainless steel or aluminum, or so-called heat exchangers that are made of aluminum. All of these are qualified to use, given that hot water and steam are produced at the right temperature. Since optimum quality water is another key ingredient for brewing a top quality coffee, fresh and filtered water should be used and not be left in the heating systems for prolonged periods, but should be replaced daily. When the machine has not been in use for some time, it is advisable to run the pump in order to flush the system and simultaneously pre-heat the filter holder and filter basket. As described below, there are further properties, features and accessories offered in modern espresso machines, which of course also effect the price of a machine.

This does not necessarily mean that a machine has to be expensive to make a quality espresso. When shopping for a good machine, observe that it features the technical prerequisites for proper espresso brewing as explained in this book.

Casing Materials

Traditionally household espresso machines were fabricated in metal casings. Modern manufacturing has progressed to implementing high quality plastic materials for the sake of production cost. Upon customers request, there is a new trend to manufacturing in metal materials again. This is often done in the "retro look" of yesterday, with surfaces of chrome and stainless steel.

Electronic Programming

Usually the water flow and quantity in the cup is controlled by a switch which activates the pump. Some models have an electronic dosage system for the water, by which the desired amount in the cup can be preset.

Built in Grinders

A special feature on some machines is a built in grinder, which allows to grind the beans just prior to brewing. The alternative is to have a separate grinder, buy coffee pre-ground or use the most convenient choice, pre-packed portioned coffee pods.

Fully Automatic Espresso Coffee Machines

These are the latest generation of espresso machines on the market today, and they offer ultimate convenience and consistent quality at the push of a button, time after time. These sophisticated, computer generated machines generally grind, dose, tamp, brew and dispense the used coffee grounds in one simultaneous cycle and have the capability of brewing one or two cups (from one to eight ounces in size) at a time. Many of the fully featured models include an electronic module with diagnosis center, separated heated cup stacking surface, instant hot water for tea and/or hot chocolate and powerful steam for frothing milk for cappuccino and latte drinks.

What please is a "Portafilter"?

A handle on espresso brewing.

The word is Italian for filter holder and describes the device that is used to fix the filter basket with the coffee powder into the espresso machine. That's what the traditional filter holder does.

There are various types of filter holders available today and now some come equipped with special extraction devices and the newest generation is even able to accommodate the Easy Serving Espresso pods.

The traditional filter holder consists of a metal cup that holds the filter basket and is mounted to a handle. It usually holds filters that allow it to make one or two shots of espresso and that's why they have two dispensing spigots at the bottom.

State of the art filter holders are pressurized by means of an integrated valve. A minimum of 120 psi is required to open this valve. Since correct pressure is the essence for good quality espresso, these devices assure optimum results every time. It is important to make sure that the filter holder is hot when brewing coffee. This can be achieved either by leaving it on the heated machine, or attaching it to the machine and flushing it shortly by operating the pump.

Kisses
sweeter than...

Perfect milk froth with ease.

The traditional way of frothing milk requires a stainless steel pitcher. Other similar dishes or containers may be used, but will not serve as well. Further to the earlier described traditional method of frothing milk, there are handy accessories that use a jet-stream like technology to make perfect froth every time. Two of the major accessories are described below.

The **Pannarello** is a frother device that will fit on most of the common modern espresso machines available. It is especially useful to froth smaller quantities of milk in a pitcher or a cup and ensures a firm and stable milk froth.

The **Cappuccinatore** is derived from the so-called "Venturi-Effect". The steam pressure creates a vacuum that sucks the cold milk into a chamber and in the process aerates it into froth. This method and device is especially good for frothing larger quantities of milk.

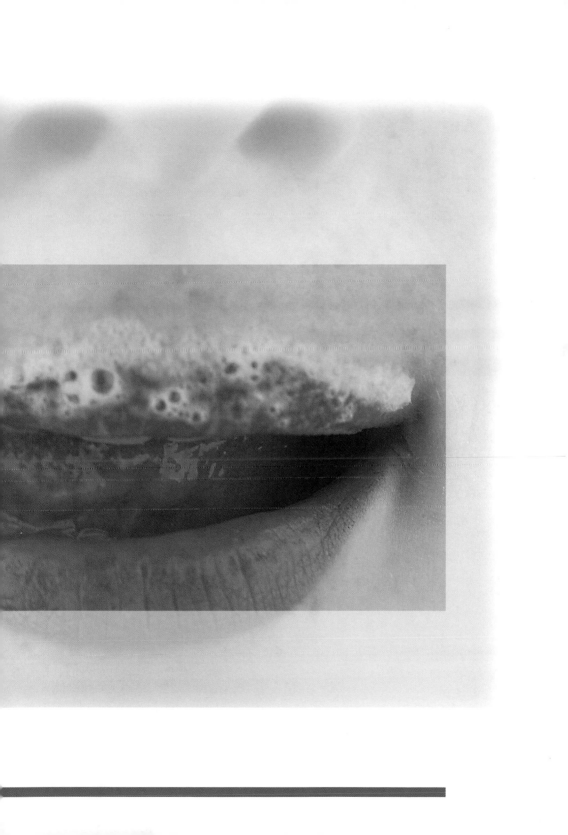

...and Co

Ristretto - The smallest is the strongest

The "little one" in the family is typical to Southern Italy. It is made with the same amount of coffee powder as regular espresso, but with less water. Thus it is restricted and therefore called "ristretto".

Caffè Espresso - The Classic

The methodology for a good quality espresso has been discussed at length previously. All it really takes is good equipment, 7 grams of a fine blend, pure water and a lot of passion. It's the coffee's heart and soul – and every time you see it, you'll recognize it!

Espresso and espresso based coffee specialities.

It is the dark Italian roast, brewed in an espresso machine as an intense, concentrated extract, that is Italy's gift to the world of coffee and the basis of many of today's coffee drinks.

Caffé Lungo - A long espresso

An espresso prepared with a little more water in Italy is called a long coffee. Isn't it nice to be able to tell the barista what kind of an extraction you prefer?

Café Crème - The regular guy from Switzerland

Gone are the days of drip filter coffee in quality conscious Switzerland. A fully automatic espresso system belongs to the standard of an average household. Although the majority of coffee drinks are not the short Italian espressi, but the regular size cup of coffee, brewed by utilizing the superior espresso method and called Café Crème.

Co

Caffè Latte - The breakfast drink

A double espresso in a tall glass topped with
hot milk without or only little foam. This drink
is fast becoming an American favorite.

Café Au Lait - The French cousin

Maybe just because the French sometimes
don't take life too seriously, it may there occa-
sionally be served also made from drip filter
coffee, but we really prefer it with a double
shot espresso and the same amount of hot
milk, served in a "bol", the typical French dish.

Caffè Macchiato - The speckled one

Some hot milk with foam is added to the espresso and because of this way of preparation it sometimes becomes a little speckled and so it received its Italian name.

Cappuccino - America's favorite coffee drink

The classic cappuccino calls for equal quantities of espresso, milk and milk froth with no cream. A nice addition is some coca powder sprinkled on top of the frothed milk.

Co

Viennese Cappuccino - The Austrian delight

This drink is made with a long espresso and some hot milk, topped with whipped cream and some chocolate bits.

Caffè Corretto - Good reason for good brandy

Italians learned long ago that their favorite drink, the espresso, could be spiced up with the addition of grappa, brandy or their liqueur of choice.

Ice Coffee - Fire and Ice

Two scoops of vanilla ice cream in a tall glass
with whipped cream.
Top it off with an espresso lungo and add some
more cream and chocolate bits for decoration.
Beware of imitations with filter coffee.

Glossary & Tools.

Aroma

The flavor of freshly brewed coffee fills the air and it is an indescribable and unique delight, which only can be surpassed by drinking it. Smelling and tasting combined are the Aroma which we sense. Smelling can absorb a lot of aroma, whereas the full delight is in the tasting of the coffee.

Storage

Ground coffee is subject to loosing its aroma faster than whole beans. Oxygen, humidity and unwanted flavors have a negative effect. Therefore, coffee needs to be stored in a cool and dry location. Always keep coffee in the refrigerator.

Barista (plural: baristi)

They are the artists and members of a highly regarded profession in Italy. They serve in the typical Italian coffee bars. They know their machine, know all the coffee specialties and are always striving to serve their customers a perfect drink.

Crema

It surely does not deserve to be called foam. The crema contains the essence of extraction and is created by pressure through the brewing process, as described throughout the book. Who really wants to find out what it is, should take an espresso spoon with a little bit of sugar, scoop the crema from the top of the espresso and enjoy the succulent experience.

Mocha Maker

Some manufacturers try to imply that cheap machines without a pump would be espresso machines. Without a pump classical espresso can not be made. Such machines should more correctly be called mocha makers.

Pressure

Espresso brewing calls for pressure created by a pump. The pressure of steam is only to be used to froth milk. Steam pressure driven machines burn the coffee and deprive it from its true quality.

Espresso spoons
The perfect cup deserves the perfect spoon. Regular spoons are too big for serving espresso and a specially made espresso spoon should be on hand. These small spoons are of a size that fits the espresso cup. Regular spoons are suitable for those drinks that are being served in larger cups.

Extraction
This word describes the qualitative and quantitative release of aroma and related substances. The blend, grind, water temperature, pressure and contact time of water and coffee powder make up the major parameters that determine the result of the extraction.

The ultimate goal is perfect extraction, but there are also over-extraction and under-extraction. The crema of an over-extracted espresso is too dark,

with either a white spot or a hole in the middle. The reason usually is too hot brewing or too much compressed coffee powder from a too fine grind. Under-extracted coffee shows a too light crema, which is of weak consistency and dissipates quickly. The reason for that is too coarse grinding, too low temperature or not tamping the coffee.

Health and coffee
Although there is much controversy on the subject, it is a laboratory proven fact that espresso only contains about half of the caffeine and acids that may affect health, as is contained in the same amount of regular filter coffee. At the same time the coffee drinker values the vitalizing and stimulating effects of a good cup of coffee.

Caffeine and other substances
Coffee contains about 1,000 substances, of which about 800 are related to aroma. The most well-known substance probably is caffeine. According to today's state of science, it is generally recognized to be harmless if consumed in sensible amounts by healthy people.

Other important substances are carbon hydrates, fat, water, protein, acids and minerals.

Decaffeinated Espresso
In selected stores it is also possible to find decaffeinated espresso beans. These are actually up to the quality standard of regular espresso beans and it's basically impossible to tell the difference.

under-extraction | over-extraction

Glossary & Tools

Grinder
The modern espresso grinders are equipped with hardened metal burrs. Blade grinders are not suggested, since they destroy the flavor by the speed of the blades creating too much heat.

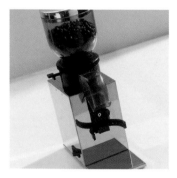

Stove Top Mocha Maker
One of the early predecessors of today's espresso machines. It extracts with too much heat though to be honestly called an espresso.

Portioning
One measuring spoon is equal to 7 grams of coffee powder. This amount is ideal for one cup of espresso.

Milk Frothing Pitcher
Pitchers of stainless steel serve best to froth milk. They must be large enough for the purpose, as the frothing milk expands considerably.

Tamper
A handheld device that is used to lightly tamp the coffee powder into the filter basket. This is expertly done with a 90 degree circular motion.
Some espresso machines and grinders feature a built in tamper.

Provinces
Geographical term for areas, in this meaning regions where coffee is cultivated.

French Press
There is probably no device that makes preparing a respectably good coffee more easy. It is not an espresso, but one can influence heat and contact time more than with drip coffee machines.

Espresso and Cappuccino cups
Cups play a major role in the espresso coffee culture. Just as it is important to drink wine from the right glases, it is imperative for the real connoisseur to serve specialty coffees in the right dishes. Specially made espresso cups need to be preheated to ensure the right temperature of the drink. The aesthetics of the cup enhances the pleasure of the drink to perfection.

Toppings
Classical toppings are shaved chocolate, chocolate bits and coffee powder. But everyone should feel free to experiment with toppings of their choice.

Sugar
Granulated sugar is a must. It can be white sugar, brown sugar or a special mixture of both. Never use sugar cubes or any solid form, as the undesirable stirring will destroy the valued crema. Although some people prefer to drink their espresso without sugar, it generally is to be considered an enhancing element to the quality of a truly great espresso.